The Ta...

Christopher Hampton was born in the Azores in 1946. He wrote his first play, *When Did You Last See My Mother?* at the age of eighteen. Since then, his plays have included *The Philanthropist, Savages, Tales from Hollywood, Les Liaisons Dangereuses, White Chameleon* and *The Talking Cure.* He has translated plays by Ibsen, Molière, von Horváth, Chekhov and Yasmina Reza (including *Art* and *Life x 3*). His television work includes adaptations of *The History Man* and *Hotel du Lac.* His screenplays include *The Honorary Consul, The Good Father, Dangerous Liaisons, Mary Reilly, Total Eclipse, The Quiet American, Carrington, The Secret Agent* and *Imagining Argentina*, the last three of which he also directed.

by the same author

CHRISTOPHER HAMPTON PLAYS I
(*The Philanthropist, Total Eclipse, Savages, Treats*)

LES LIAISONS DANGEREUSES
WHITE CHAMELEON
TALES FROM HOLLYWOOD

screenplays

COLLECTED SCREENPLAYS
(*Dangerous Liaisons, Carrington, Mary Reilly,
A Bright Shining Lie, The Custom of the Country*)

TOTAL ECLIPSE
THE SECRET AGENT & NOSTROMO

translations

Yasmina Reza's
ART
THE UNEXPECTED MAN
CONVERSATIONS AFTER A BURIAL
LIFE X 3

CHRISTOPHER HAMPTON

The Talking Cure

faber and faber

First published in 2002
by Faber and Faber Limited
3 Queen Square London WC1N 3AU
Published in the United States by Faber and Faber Inc.
an affiliate of Farrar, Straus and Giroux LLC, New York

Typeset by Country Setting, Kingsdown, Kent CT14 8ES
Printed by CPI Antony Rowe, Eastbourne

Christopher Hampton is hereby identified as author
of this work in accordance with Section 77 of the
Copyright, Designs and Patents Act 1988

A CIP record for this book
is available from the British Library

ISBN 978-0-571-21485-3

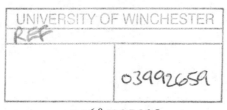
2 4 6 8 10 9 7 5 3 1

The Talking Cure was first presented at the Royal
National Theatre, London, on 6 December 2002, with
the following cast:

Carl Gustav Jung Ralph Fiennes
Emma Jung Nancy Carroll
Sabina Spielrein Jodhi May
Nurse Valerie Spelman
Sigmund Freud James Hazeldine
Otto Gross Dominic Rowan
Orderly/SS Officer Sean Jackson

Director Howard Davies
Set Designer Tim Hatley
Costume Designer Jenny Beavan
Lighting Designer Peter Mumford
Music Dominic Muldowney
Sound Designer Christopher Shutt

Characters

Carl Gustav Jung
Emma Jung
Sabina Spielrein
Sigmund Freud
Otto Gross

An Orderly
A Nurse
A Russian Girl (six years old)
An S.S. Officer
Agathe Jung (six/eight years old)

Locations

Act One

SCENE ONE

The living room of the apartment assigned to the assistant director of the Burghölzli Hospital in Zürich: Dr Carl Gustav Jung, a tall, broad, godlike young man of twenty-nine with a high collar, steel-rimmed glasses and a sensible moustache, who is taking coffee with his wife Emma, an attractive twenty-two-year-old, now five months pregnant. It's 17 August 1904, and outside, a summer storm flickers and grumbles. After a moment of companionable silence, Jung turns to Emma.

Jung The case history I was writing up last week; you remember I chose the code name Sabina S?

Emma Yes.

Jung This evening we admitted a new patient, a Russian. Her name is Sabina Spielrein.

Emma What a coincidence.

Jung Yes; except, as you know, I don't believe there is such a thing.

Pause. Emma puts down her cup.

Emma Perhaps she's the one.

Jung What one?

Emma The one you've been waiting for. To try out your new treatment: the talking cure.

Jung considers for a moment.

Jung You know, she might very well fill the bill. An hysteric. Extremely well educated.

Emma Speaks good German?

Jung Absolutely fluent.

Emma Not a very Russian name.

Jung No: more Jewish. Father's a big, crude-looking fellow with a red face. Very successful businessman, apparently. Quite rich.

Emma Rich?

Jung So I gathered.

Emma Then why's he brought her to the public asylum?

Jung She was at Dr Heller's sanatorium in Interlaken. It seems she threw quite a lot of furniture out of the windows without bothering to open them first. After which, none of the other private hospitals would take her.

Emma Is she violent?

Jung That's what they say: but so far she's just been shouting a good deal, roaring with laughter and sticking her tongue out at people.

Emma How old is she?

Jung Eighteen, nineteen.

Emma Sounds ideal. (*She puts her cup on the tray, moves to collect Jung's, then hesitates.*) He's kicking: can you feel?

> *Jung rests his hand for a moment on her stomach.*

Jung Yes, there he is.

> *He reflects, as Emma continues tidying up.*

Don't you think it's odd that, having proposed this radical therapeutic idea, Freud then lets years go by without describing any kind of methodology, not even the barest outline of his clinical procedures? What's he playing at?

Emma But he does use the method himself on his patients?

Jung I assume so. I've no idea.

Emma So you might be the first doctor to try this out?

Jung I wouldn't think so.

Emma What's it called?

Jung Psychanalysis.

Emma Why don't you write to him and ask him?

Jung What, out of the blue?

Emma Why not?

Jung I don't know him. (*He thinks for a moment, then smiles at Emma.*) I'll see if it works first.

SCENE TWO

In the centre of a bare, white room, a specially prepared consulting room at the Burghölzli, Sabina Spielrein sits alone, bolt upright on a straight-backed chair. She's a slight, beautiful, olive-skinned young woman of eighteen, wearing a simple dress, her dark hair braided into a single plait which reaches down to her waist. Her pretty face is deformed by a series of savagely violent tics. The room is dimly lit, its windows darkened with blinds. There's one other chair in the room, five or six feet behind Sabina and slightly to one side.

After a while, Sabina looks up, her expression hunted. She's heard the approach of Jung; she looks away as he breezes into the room.

Jung Good morning, I'm Dr Jung, the assistant director of the hospital; and you're to be my patient.

By now he's standing in front of her, his hand outstretched. She looks at him through narrowed eyes, won't take his hand. He resumes, apparently not in the least discouraged.

How are you feeling?

Sabina I'm not mad, you know.

Jung No.

Sabina It's just that I couldn't stand that other hotel.

Jung I hope you'll be more comfortable here. Did you sleep all right?

Sabina They wouldn't let me keep the light on.

Jung You like to sleep with the light on?

Sabina I . . . (*Her mouth stays open, she seems to be making a great effort to speak, but no sound is coming out.*)

Jung I see no reason why that shouldn't be allowed.

Sabina closes her mouth, relief in her eyes.

Is there anything else you want to say to me?

Sabina My body, my body; my body is someone else. It has two heads.

Jung nods, almost imperceptibly, his expression sympathetic. Then he straightens up, to his full, imposing height.

Jung Let me explain what I have in mind: I propose that we meet here, most days, to talk for an hour or two.

Sabina Talk?

4

Jung Yes. Just talk. See if we can identify whatever it is that's troubling you. So as to distract you as little as possible, I shall sit there, behind you; and I'm going to ask you to try not to turn round and look at me under any circumstances.

He moves behind her and sits in the second chair. Her face twitches, her expression is apprehensive.

Now. You're from . . .

Sabina Rostov. Rostov-na-Donu.

Jung I don't know Russia.

Sabina It's not what you imagine when you think of Russia. It's a beautiful city. On the Black Sea.

Jung How do you come to speak such perfect German?

Sabina It was one of my subjects. At the grammar school. I just graduated.

Jung Hm. I'm afraid in Switzerland we never educate our young women up to your level, as a matter of principle.

Sabina I don't know if you could call it education, the teachers were so incredibly stupid.

Jung has opened a small notebook on his knee; he makes a note, as he is to do throughout these scenes in the consulting room.

Jung Have you some idea of what may have brought on these attacks you suffer from?

Sabina, taken by surprise by the directness of this question, has to struggle for some time before she can answer.

Sabina Humiliation.

Silence. Jung waits, his attention tightly concentrated. Sabina's head jerks back and rotates in a massive involuntary tic.

Any kind of . . . humiliation or victimisation, I can't bear to watch it. It makes me feel nauseous, I start pouring with sweat, cold sweat; then I have to go to bed for days.

Jung No one likes to see that kind of thing. But these must have been isolated incidents?

Long silence; Sabina is in obvious distress. Finally, Jung risks a gentle prompt.

Were they not?

Sabina No, often, they were often, happened often.

Jung Was this at home?

Sabina My . . . father lost his temper all the time, he was always angry: with my brothers.

Jung With your brothers?

Sabina Mmm.

Jung Not with you?

Sabina Sometimes, ah . . . sometimes. But mostly with my brothers.

Jung What would he do?

Sabina Shout and . . . shout. And hit them. (*By now she's writhing in her chair, her leg twitching, her face out of control.*)

Jung But you do love your father?

Sabina Ah, yes, but I couldn't . . . I couldn't . . . he was so sad sometimes and I wasn't able to . . . pride . . . it was the most painful kind of love . . . I . . .

She breaks off. Jung waits.

I couldn't even . . .

Jung Yes?

Sabina . . . speak French to him . . .

Jung Speak French?

Sabina Yes, I was . . . studying French and I used to come downstairs, I would say *bonjour* to everyone, but I couldn't, I couldn't . . . not to him . . . I couldn't . . . kiss him . . . (*Her head starts jerking violently.*)

Jung When you paused just now, what were you thinking about?

Sabina When?

Jung Just now: you stopped in the middle of what you were saying. Did a thought come into your head?

Sabina I don't . . . ah . . .

Jung Or an image perhaps? Was it an image?

Sabina Yes, an image . . . yes.

Jung What was the image?

Sabina A hand. (*She writhes in her chair during a long silence; finally, she comes to rest and speaks very quietly.*) My father's hand.

Jung speaks as quietly, anxious not to break the spell.

Jung Why do you think you saw that?

Sabina After he . . . whenever he hit us . . . afterwards . . .

Jung Yes?

Sabina We had to kiss his hand.

She twists and turns in her chair. Jung writes in his notebook.

The apartment: Emma sits, calmly watching Jung as he paces around the room, deep in thought, a glass of water in his hand.

Jung Then I talked to her mother.

Emma Oh, yes? What's she like?

Jung Chilly. She's a dentist.

Emma Ouch.

Jung Says she loves her work, with a sinister glint in her eye. Complained about Sabina's illnesses.

Emma The hysteria?

Jung No, no, physical illnesses. Diphtheria, scarlet fever, everything you can think of. Constipation.

Emma Poor thing.

Jung She spoke very disparagingly of Sabina's excess of compassion, you know, her feeling for beggars, her worrying about peasants starving in the Caucasus. She said Sabina wanted to be a doctor, as if she were describing some particularly unfortunate adolescent fad.

Emma Doesn't sound very sympathetic.

Jung She said Sabina was too clever by half, and an intellectual snob who was incapable of talking to ordinary people. (*He shakes his head and drains off his glass of water.*) I need a drink.

Emma I'm sorry.

Jung It's a ridiculous rule; what does the Herr Direktor think we're going to do, hold bacchanalian orgies in the refectory? (*He refills his glass from the water carafe.*)

8

Emma But the treatment went well?

Jung I think so; I don't know. It was certainly extremely interesting. But my instinct is, I did too much talking.

Emma Hard to imagine.

She's clearly teasing him; but at the moment he's too self-absorbed to notice.

Jung I have to find a way to say less; to intervene less.

SCENE FOUR

Sabina's private room at the Burghölzli; it's night, and Sabina sits on the bed in her nightdress. She looks up as a brightly smiling Nurse, not much older than she is, lets herself into the room.

Nurse Bedtime!

Sabina Oh. Could you just give me five minutes?

She rises to her feet as she speaks: the Nurse, still smiling, shakes her head.

Nurse No, no: we have to keep to our timetable.

There's a screened-off section in the corner of the room with jug, bowl and chamber pot: Sabina gestures in its direction.

Sabina I just want to use the . . .

Nurse Go ahead.

Sabina Can't I have five minutes' privacy?

Nurse Good heavens, don't worry about me! Off you go. I'll wait.

She's still smiling infuriatingly. There's a pause; Sabina's eyes dart around the room.

9

Sabina In that case, I prefer to kill myself.

With tremendous speed, she flashes across to the window, wrenches the curtain out of the wall, extricates the cord which holds up the curtain and wraps it around her neck. The Nurse, initially caught by surprise and slow to react, is now grappling with her. Eventually, she manages to unwrap the cord and get it away from Sabina; this leaves the pocket watch attached to her uniform vulnerable and, in an instant, Sabina has ripped it off her dress, thrown it to the ground and stamped on it. As the Nurse drops to one knee to gather up the shards of her watch, Sabina seizes the glass jug of lemonade and hurls it against the wall, where it shatters noisily. By this time, the Nurse has managed to get out her whistle, which she blows, panic-stricken. Sabina sticks out her tongue at the Nurse, looking her defiantly in the eye. Presently, Jung arrives, accompanied by a burly Orderly. Sabina ignores him completely.

Jung Is something the matter, Miss Spielrein?

Sabina No.

Nurse She attacked me and . . .

Jung raises a hand, silencing her: he turns back to Sabina.

Jung Now, what's been happening?

Sabina I just . . . wanted to answer a call of nature, so I asked for five minutes' privacy. She wouldn't give it to me.

Nurse She threw the jug of lemonade at me; she stamped on my watch, look.

Jung Is this true, Miss Spielrein?

Sabina Yes. (*She bursts into raucous laughter.*)

Jung Will you go to bed now, please?

She stops laughing abruptly.

Sabina Certainly.

She gets up calmly and pulls back the covers on her bed. Jung turns to the Nurse and the Orderly.

Jung I think we should leave Miss Spielrein.

As he begins to shepherd them towards the exit, Sabina, now in bed, speaks in a very passable imitation of Jung's voice.

Sabina Now are you quite sure you didn't say anything to upset the patient?

Jung, surprised, stifles a smile.

Jung Good night, Miss Spielrein.

The Nurse is unable to suppress her indignation a moment longer.

Nurse She threatened to kill herself.

Sabina It was that or threatening to kill you.

Jung That's enough, Miss Spielrein: now do as you're told.

Sabina looks at him, lips apart, a strange expression on her face.

SCENE FIVE

The consulting room: Sabina sits on her chair in her nightdress, wrapped in an old grey blanket. Jung is in his position, behind her, notebook open on his knee.

Sabina You want suicide attempts, it's my father you should have in here.

Jung Go on.

Sabina My father's always threatening suicide, it's one of his techniques when one or other of us . . . disappoints him. One of these days I'm afraid he'll really do it. He thinks my mother doesn't love him . . . and he's right, she doesn't.

Jung But you, have you never felt suicidal?

Sabina Once, in Karlsbad, I went on a hunger strike . . . and another time I lay down in the snow, thinking I could give myself pneumonia. But no, no . . . except when my little sister died . . .

Silence. Jung waits. In front of him, Sabina shudders, her head jerks to and fro.

She had typhus. She was six. It was three years ago. I loved her more than anything in the world.

She lowers her head. Huge tears start to roll down her cheeks. Jung waits, motionless. Eventually, Sabina raises her head.

From the time I was seven, my mother always told me I was fully responsible for my sins.

Jung And this worried you?

Sabina Terribly. But then the angel came and everything was all right.

Jung What angel?

Sabina An inner voice. I decided it was the voice of an angel. He told me I was an exceptional person. He always spoke in German.

Jung Then he must have been an angel.

Sabina Do angels always speak German?

Jung It's traditional.

Sabina smiles, perhaps for the first time.

Sabina He gave me the power to know what people were going to say before they opened their mouths.

Jung Do you still have that power?

Sabina Sometimes.

Jung Useful ability for a doctor.

Sabina I'll never be a doctor.

She jerks convulsively and the blanket slips from her shoulders to the floor. For a moment, Jung doesn't move; then his Swiss desire for order gets the better of him and he rises and picks up the blanket. Noticing it's dusty, he holds it away from him and slaps at it a couple of times. Then he notices Sabina is looking up at him in horror.

Don't do that.

Jung I was just . . .

Sabina Stop it!

Jung I'm sorry.

He drops the blanket and returns to his seat. Sabina is trembling, her face contorted.

Sabina Oh, what do you care? You don't have time for any of this. (*She's looking angry now, her voice is full of indignation.*) I want to go back, I can't tell you whatever it is you want to know, this is a waste of time, you're just making me angry . . . If I was to tell you, you'd be sorry you ever . . . (*She straightens up; her voice goes cold.*) I don't want to talk any more. There's nothing wrong with me! I don't even want to get better!

Jung doesn't react or speak. And suddenly Sabina swings round in her chair to glare at him furiously. He looks at her for a while, then gently shakes his head. For a moment she maintains her position; then, slowly, she turns back and looks ahead again, her expression insecure, fear in her eyes.

SCENE SIX

The apartment: Jung is slumped dejectedly in an armchair; Emma moves serenely to and fro, engaged on some domestic task.

Jung If you want a professional army, have a professional army; don't dragoon a lot of clerks and shopkeepers two weeks a year who don't know left from right and couldn't shoot an elephant at three paces.

Emma You're right.

Jung It's a complete waste of my time. Writing prescriptions for athlete's foot and examining people's cocks from morning to night.

Emma Is that what you do?

Jung I spent ten days with her, there was an enormous improvement; then I get back and find she's gone completely off the rails.

Emma I heard rumours.

Jung She escaped from the building and was found at the top of a ladder, refusing to come down; she wouldn't take a bath, until they had to bath her forcibly; she blocked all the hallways with benches; she called the Herr Direktor an old goat; and she stole a knife and pinned this message to the notice board. (*He brings a piece of paper out of his pocket.*)

Emma What does it say?

Jung It says: 'If I'm not here tomorrow, it doesn't necessarily mean that I'm dead.' She also refused to eat for two days, on the grounds that nobody eats on the planet Mars. (*He sighs exasperatedly.*) I'll just have to start from scratch, that's all.

Emma Are you going to persist with your method? (*She stops in her tracks, waiting for the answer.*)

Jung I am. I most certainly am.

SCENE SEVEN

Jung leads Sabina into the consulting room, holding her hand. She's walking with the greatest difficulty, balancing on the outside edge of both feet. He leads her to her chair and helps her to sit down. Then he moves to and fro behind her back, not sitting down for the moment, thinking.

Jung Tell me where it hurts.

Sabina The bottom . . . the balls of my feet.

Jung The soles.

Sabina Whatever you say.

Jung How long has this been troubling you?

Sabina Ever since that day I left the building and walked around the grounds.

Jung continues pacing for a while; then, eventually, he takes his seat and speaks quietly.

Jung Tell me: has anything like this ever happened to you before?

Sabina Once.

Jung waits through a long silence.

They were having one of their fights, can't remember what
about, just one of their . . . he got so angry, he went to
bed, didn't speak or eat for two days . . . then some
neighbour comes to call and she makes me go upstairs to
my father and tell him he has to get up, we have to keep
up appearances . . . so he did get up and we had tea
and then we all went out for a walk as if nothing had
happened and everything was . . . normal and we were
a normal family and halfway through I . . . it happened
and I couldn't walk any more and they had to carry me
home . . . (*Her head drops and there's another extended
silence.*)

Jung What was it about being out in the grounds that
reminded you of this incident?

Sabina I just . . . it's the first time I've been outside
since . . . I started to think, I can't stay here for ever,
I have to go out sometime, go back, I mean, and I'm . . .
afraid, afraid of leaving, afraid of the future, afraid of . . .

*She breaks off; and this time Jung doesn't wait before
speaking.*

Jung We won't let you out until we know you're ready
to go. So please don't worry on that score.

*Silence. Sabina closes her eyes. Then she stretches out
her left hand at shoulder height.*

Sabina I want you to take my hand.

*Jung hesitates; he's not sure what to do. Then he rises,
steps forward and lightly takes her hand.*

Yes. Now I want you to squeeze it. I want you to squeeze
till it really hurts. Then I might be able to tell you
something.

In his uncertainty, Jung does nothing. Sabina grits her teeth.

You're very strong. If you wanted to, you could break every bone in my hand. (*She turns her head away and braces herself.*) Do it.

Nothing happens.

Do it! Please!

Jung lets go of her hand, as he knows he should have ten seconds earlier. Sabina groans; her head drops to her chest. Jung goes back to his seat. Then he speaks, calmly and quietly.

Jung Normally, with my patients, I use a method of my own called the word-association test. It's still at an experimental stage, but it's yielded some very encouraging results. For various reasons, in your case I've chosen a different technique, but since you're interested in medical procedures and since we're extremely short-staffed, I'm wondering if you'd care to assist me with some of my experiments?

Sabina's head comes up, very slowly. Her eyes are shining.

SCENE EIGHT

Jung's office in the Burghölzli: another plain room. Emma, noticeably more pregnant, sits in a straight-backed chair, hooked up to an electro-galvanometer; Jung, holding a clipboard, is seated at an angle so that he can monitor the galvanometer; and Sabina sits off to one side, with a notebook and a stopwatch.

Jung Vienna.

Emma Woods.

17

Jung Box.

Emma Bed.

Jung Money.

Emma Bank.

Jung Child.

> *Emma hesitates: Jung leans forward to inspect the dial on the galvanometer, which has registered some movement.*

Emma Soon.

Jung Family.

> *Longer pause. Sabina activates her stopwatch.*

Emma Unit.

Jung Sex.

Emma Er, male.

Jung Wall.

Emma Flower.

Jung Young.

> *Another pause: another reaction on the galvanometer.*

Emma Baby.

Jung Ask.

Emma Answer.

Jung Cap.

Emma Wear.

Jung Stubborn.

Emma Give way.

Jung Ruefulness.

Sabina records about ten seconds on the stopwatch.

Emma Child.

Jung Fame.

Emma Doctor.

Jung Divorce.

Another long pause; the galvanometer is clearly reacting wildly, and Sabina watches the hand ticking away on the stopwatch.

Emma No.

Jung relaxes with a warm smile and disconnects Emma from the machine.

Jung Thank you.

Emma Is that all?

Jung That's all.

Slightly surprised, Emma heaves herself to her feet and crosses to the door.

Goodbye.

Emma Erm, yes. Goodbye.

She leaves the room. After a moment, Jung turns to Sabina.

Jung Any preliminary observations?

Sabina Well, obviously what's uppermost in her mind is her pregnancy.

Jung Good.

Sabina She's a little . . . what's the word?

Jung Why don't we try a useful word invented by the Herr Direktor: ambivalent?

Sabina Yes . . . about the baby, I mean.

Jung Anything else?

Sabina I'd say she was worried her husband might be losing interest in her.

Jung What makes you think that?

Sabina Long reaction times to the words 'family' and 'divorce'.

Jung I see.

Sabina And when you said 'cap', she said 'wear'. Could that be a reference to contraception?

Jung smiles, impressed.

Jung You have quite a flair for this.

Sabina Can I ask you something?

Jung Of course. What?

Sabina Is she your wife?

Jung is taken by surprise; but he soon recovers and nods, smiling.

SCENE NINE

The consulting room: Jung and Sabina sit in their habitual positions, at the moment in silence; and from Sabina's hunched, uncomfortable position and the grimace made by Jung as he uncrosses his legs, they would seem to have been there for some time. Eventually, Sabina breaks the silence.

Sabina Can we stop now?

Jung I'd like to go on a little longer.

Sabina But hasn't it been . . . I mean, how long has it been?

Jung We've been talking for about two and a half hours.

Sabina Then why can't we . . .?

Jung takes a moment before answering.

Jung It's nearly five months since we started these sessions; and a pattern has been established. You show continuing improvement; and then, as a result of factors we can sometimes identify, but which often remain mysterious, you fall back. It's my belief that there's one step more to be taken; and as we're here, our first session of the New Year, I have a sense that progress is possible.

Sabina Wouldn't you be better off spending some time with your baby?

Jung I hope she'll be asleep by now.

Sabina I haven't congratulated you.

Jung The whole event was very low key. I managed to smuggle a bottle of champagne past the Herr Direktor. Now, shall we resume?

Silence. A first tic skitters across Sabina's face.

Sabina I don't know what to tell you.

Jung waits a moment before his next decisive intervention.

Jung Why don't we go back to the incident just before Christmas, when we went shopping in Zurich? Everything was going so well, then you suddenly became distressed;

and finally you tried to attack that woman in the fur coat. Did she remind you of your mother?

Sabina No, shopping, the word shopping, it was when you . . . spoke the word.

Jung Why did that upset you?

Sabina takes a breath, as if to fend off panic.

Sabina Whenever . . . things got really bad at home, my mother would go shopping. She only bought things we didn't need, she'd buy anything, as long as it was expensive and useless. Then she'd have to hide it from my father and borrow money from her friends and try to pay them back out of her allowance, all the time terrified he'd find out, and so I . . . (*She breaks off abruptly.*)

Jung Did he ever find out?

Sabina Once. He had a screaming fit and broke everything. It was like the end of the world.

Jung Well, now I understand. And you say that since the incident in Zürich you haven't been able to sleep. Can you explain?

Sabina I'm afraid.

Jung Of what?

Sabina Something, there's something in the room . . . something like a cat, only it . . . can speak, it gets into bed with me.

Long silence. Jung waits.

Last, last night, it suddenly whispered something in my ear, I couldn't hear what . . . but then . . . I felt it behind me . . . it put its hand on my waist and then . . . (*She's twisting furiously in her chair, in an agony of discomfort.*) . . . I felt something against my back, something slimy like some kind of a . . . mollusc . . . moving against my back, but when I turned round there was nothing there.

Jung You felt it against your back?

Sabina Yes.

Jung Were you naked?

Sabina I was.

Jung Were you masturbating?

Sabina Yes.

There's another long silence. Jung seems about to break it, when Sabina speaks again.

Anyway, I loathe New Years . . .

Jung sits up, suddenly alert.

Jung Why?

Sabina All those fights at home: for example, last New Year's Day, he got into a terrible rage, nobody could understand why, it was something my brother Isaac said . . . and . . . and . . . he . . .

A tremendous barrage of tics and writhing limbs overwhelms her for a moment.

. . . beat him . . . in front of everyone . . . and I . . . I . . .

She can't go on. Jung waits a while before intervening.

Jung We've talked a lot about these outbursts of your father's. Tell me about the worst one you can remember involving you.

Sabina struggles helplessly with her unruly body for a while; then she manages to begin speaking.

Sabina I must have been about thirteen . . . yes, I was thirteen . . . he got angry about something. He . . . took me into that special little room and . . . told me to bend over the bed and lift my dress up so he could . . . beat me . . . and I wouldn't do it, I told him I was too old and finally he . . . gave in and made me kneel down and kiss my grandfather's picture and swear on his memory that I would always be a . . . good girl . . . a good girl . . .

Silence.

Jung And that was the worst time?

Sabina Yes . . . I . . .

Jung Even though he didn't beat you?

Sabina Yes, as far as I . . .

Jung Because there were times, weren't there, when he did beat you?

Sabina Oh, yes, often, he often . . .

Jung Tell me about those.

Sabina's eyes are darting from place to place, she looks trapped and panicky.

Sabina Can we stop?

Jung I'd like to go on just a little longer.

Sabina So . . . ah . . . (*She struggles to control herself.*) What was your question?

Jung Tell me about the first time you can remember being beaten by your father?

For a moment it looks as if Sabina is about to be propelled out of her chair. Finally, she succeeds in speaking.

Sabina I must have . . . I suppose I was about four . . . I broke a plate . . . or . . . yes . . . and he told me to go in the little room and . . . take my clothes off . . . then he came in and . . . spanked me . . . I was so frightened I wet myself, so he . . . hit me again and . . .

Jung And after that first time, did he beat you a lot?

Sabina Oh, yes . . . yes . . . and sometimes, when he was away, my mother beat me . . . but that wasn't at all . . . it wasn't the same as . . . (*She breaks off: tears are starting to roll down her cheeks.*)

Jung And that first time, how did you feel about what was happening?

There's a long silence; after which Sabina's reply is scarcely audible.

Sabina I liked it.

Jung Would you repeat that, please? I couldn't quite hear.

Sabina I liked it. It excited me.

Jung And did you continue to like it?

Sabina gives a long groan, before she can continue speaking.

Sabina Yes . . . yes . . . before long he only had to say to me to . . . go into the little room and I would . . . start to get wet . . .

Jung And did you sometimes provoke him deliberately?

Sabina No, I . . . it happened often enough . . . and anyway . . .

She breaks off: Jung waits.

. . . whenever he beat one of my brothers . . . or even just threatened . . . that was enough . . . I'd have to go and lie down and touch myself . . . (*She cries out, as her body jolts uncontrollably up and down on the chair.*) . . . Later, at school . . . anything might set it off, if anyone

25

laughed at me . . . any kind of . . . humiliation . . . I
looked for any humiliation . . . anything . . . even here . . .
I saw one of the nurses pushing a patient into her
room . . . or when you said . . . once when you said . . .
I had to do as I was told . . . right away I had to . . .
and that time in here . . . when you beat the dust out
of that blanket, do you remember? . . . I couldn't wait
to get to my room . . . I was so excited . . .

*A torrent of sobbing plays itself out: then she's still for
a moment and her voice is quiet.*

There's no hope for me, I'm vile and filthy and corrupt,
I must never be let out of here . . .

Jung I have to ask you one more question.

*Sabina raises her head, her face still, her expression
resigned.*

Jung When you masturbate, what do you imagine? To
maintain your excitement?

Sabina Pain. Indignity. All kinds of tortures . . .

Jung Your father's hand?

Sabina Not only his: the world is full of torturers . . .

Jung And do you . . . is there a particular image that
you reserve and eventually use to bring yourself to
climax?

Sabina Yes, I . . . we're in a theatre, onstage, he rips my
clothes off and beats me in front of a huge crowd, over
his knee, all of them howling for my blood . . . howling
for my blood . . .

*Her head sinks. Long silence. Then finally, cautiously,
Jung rises to his feet.*

Jung Thank you.

*Professor Sigmund Freud's study in his apartment at
19 Berggasse, Vienna 9: it's a homely, cluttered room,
furnished in the late-Victorian style, with Turkey rugs,
a desk, neat but covered in papers, a scattering of family
photographs, a mass of classical drawings and etchings
on the wall and innumerable decorative objects, mostly
small archaeological pieces, covering every available
surface. Everything, including the books crowding the
wall of bookshelves, is in sober, dark tones.*

*Freud sits behind his desk, puffing at a cigar. He's
fifty, a slight, bearded man of medium height, carefully
and conservatively dressed in an old-fashioned frock
coat, with a shrewd and lively expression. Jung sits
opposite, on the famous couch, his legs projecting
uncomfortably off the end. It's the small hours of the
morning on 4 March 1907.*

Freud It certainly was a red-letter day when you wrote
to me about your little Russian patient. And such a
resounding success you had with her.

Jung Yes, the dramatic improvement after the initial
abreaction was like something out of a textbook. We
kept her at the hospital another few months, but it was
hardly necessary. Then we enrolled her at the University,
in the medical school, where she's doing extremely well.
A walking advertisement for the effectiveness of your
psychanalysis.

Freud Psychoanalysis.

Jung Oh?

Freud Yes, it's more logical and it sounds better. To my
ear, at least.

Jung If you say so.

Freud Are you still treating her? Your Russian?

Jung Yes; and we continue to unearth new material. For example, the other day, she told me how, between the ages of four and seven, she devised the most extraordinary procedure: she would sit on one heel, attempt to defecate, and at the same time try to prevent herself from defecating. In fact, she would sometimes go up to two weeks without defecating, all of which, she said, was accompanied by the most blissful feelings.

Freud It's a nice story. I find that those of my patients who remain fixated at the anal stage of their erotic development often come up with the most amusing details. And of course they tend to retain very similar character traits. They're finicky, compulsively tidy, stubborn and extremely stingy with money. I expect your Russian conforms to this pattern.

Jung Well, no: she doesn't.

Freud I see. (*He puffs at his cigar, evidently somewhat put out.*)

Jung As far as I can establish, the masochistic aspects of her condition are much more deeply rooted than any anal fixation we may have uncovered.

Freud But the two are intimately connected.

Jung I can only tell you she's rather disorganised, emotionally generous and exceptionally idealistic.

Freud Well: perhaps it's a Russian thing.

Jung I can tell you, she was very excited to know I was coming to Vienna to visit you. She regards you as her saviour. Indirectly.

Freud looks across at Jung, his eyes narrowed.

Freud Is she a virgin?

Jung Yes, certainly. Well, almost certainly. No, certainly.

His slight confusion is not lost on Freud, who sucks on his cigar, his good mood restored.

Freud I can't tell you how important it is to me to be able to feel confident that there will be someone, after I'm dead, to carry on with my work.

Jung Well, in a year or two, I'm sure your work will be universally accepted.

Freud shakes his head with a melancholy smile.

Freud I don't think you have any notion of the true strength and depth of the opposition to our work. There's the whole of the medical establishment, of course, that goes without saying, baying to send Freud to the *auto-da-fé*; but that's as nothing compared to what happens when our ideas begin to trickle through in whatever distorted or garbled form they're relayed to the public: the denial, the frenzy, the incoherent rage . . . you wouldn't believe it.

Jung Could it perhaps be because of your insistence on the exclusively sexual interpretation of the clinical material? Maybe if we could come up with some milder term, for instance, than 'libido', we might not encounter such obvious emotional resistance . . .

Freud I can't think that euphemism will gain us anything but the most temporary respite: once they work out what we actually mean, they'll be just as appalled as ever. All I'm doing is pointing out what experience indicates to me must be the truth . . . And I can assure you that in a hundred years' time, people will still fail to understand us, our work will still be rejected. Columbus, you know, had no idea what country he'd discovered;

like him, I'm in the dark: all I know is that I've set foot on the shore and the country exists.

Jung I think of you more as Galileo: and your opponents as those who condemned him, while refusing even to put their eye to his telescope.

Freud In any event, I've simply opened a door: it's for the young men, like yourself, to walk through it.

Jung I'm quite sure you have many more doors to open for us.

Freud At your age, I had made no mark at all: whereas you, for example, have invented the indispensable word 'complex'; even if you were run over by a bus tomorrow, you'd always be remembered for that.

Jung I hope to be remembered for more than just a single word.

Freud And I've no doubt you will be. (*He stubs out his cigar and looks across at Jung, his expression candid.*) Of course, there's the added difficulty, more ammunition for our enemies, that all of us here, in our psychoanalytical circle, happen to be Jews.

Jung I can't see what difference that makes.

Freud That, if I may say so, is an exquisitely Protestant remark. (*He lights another cigar and consults a list which is lying in front of him on the desk.*)

Freud Now: we started to discuss this dream of yours. About a horse.

Jung Yes. There's a horse, being hoisted by cables to a considerable height: in fact, there are several horses, but it's this particular large brown horse which catches my attention. Suddenly, a cable breaks and the horse is dashed to the ground. But it's not hurt, it leaps up and gallops away, impeded only by a heavy log, which it's obliged to drag along the ground. Then a rider on a small horse appears in front of it, so that it's forced to slow down; and a carriage appears in front of the small horse, so that our large horse is compelled to slow down even more.

Freud considers for a moment.

Freud I imagine the horse is yourself.

Jung Yes.

Freud And in some way your ambition has been frustrated, hence the fall.

Jung Or it may indicate a wish to strike off in my own direction.

Freud Now about this log . . .

Jung I should tell you that, because of my height, I was known in my fraternity as 'the tree'.

Freud Hm.

Jung The rider slowing me down . . .

Freud Yes.

Jung I think this refers to my wife's first pregnancy. I had to give up the opportunity to go to America because of it.

Freud Ah, America. You're right, I'm sure that's a most important territory for us.

Jung And the carriage in front slowing me still further perhaps refers to an apprehension that our two daughters, and other children perhaps still to come, will impede my progress even more.

Freud Yes, as the father of six I can vouch for that; not to mention the inevitable financial difficulties.

Jung No. Fortunately my wife is extremely rich.

Freud takes a moment to recover from this.

Freud Ah. Yes, that is fortunate. (*He frowns, turning all this over in his mind.*)

Freud This log.

Jung Yes?

Freud I think perhaps you should entertain the possibility that it represents the penis.

Jung Yes; in which case, there may be a suggestion that a certain sexual constraint has been brought about by a fear of an endless succession of pregnancies.

Freud The sexual relationship itself is, I take it, satisfactory?

Jung Entirely.

He's spoken rather too emphatically; Freud looks up at him mildly. He avoids Freud's eye and begins the elaborate process of lighting his pipe.

Freud Your interpretation seems sound enough, and, of course, you would know about this better than anyone. But I'm bound to say that if one of my patients had brought me this dream, I might have said that the number of restraining elements surrounding this unfortunate horse could perhaps point to the determined suppression of some unruly sexual desire.

Jung Yes. (*He sucks at his pipe for a while.*) Well, there is that as well.

Freud permits himself the ghost of a triumphant smile and sneaks another look at his list.

Freud Now: this young man I want you to take as a patient . . .

Jung Yes.

Freud His name is Otto Gross.

Jung I've heard of him.

Freud He's brilliant: perhaps the most brilliant young man in our field, apart, of course, from yourself. But, I'm afraid, he's extremely erratic. He's a committed immoralist, an opium addict, a cocaine addict.

Jung If he's a cocaine addict, surely you . . .

Freud interrupts him, his tone a little sharp.

Freud Yes, I follow your reasoning and indeed I only want you to supervise him for the summer, after which I'm able to take him over. I'm sure you'll find him extremely stimulating, providing you remember the warning his father used to issue to visitors when he was a child: watch out for Otto, he *bites*.

Jung Of course, I'll do what I can . . .

Freud Thank you: I think you'll find he's worth saving. (*He looks as the clock on his desk.*)

Freud I wonder if you're aware of the fact that our conversation has so far lasted thirteen hours?

Jung Good God.

Freud We'd better not start discussing Him. He's not on our list of topics.

Jung I am sorry, I had no idea . . .

Freud My dear young colleague, please don't apologise. It was our first meeting, we had a great deal to say to one another; and unless I deceive myself, we always will.

Jung nods solemnly; Freud twinkles back at him.

SCENE ELEVEN

*Jung and Sabina are leaning over the handrail on the
deck of a ferry crossing Lake Zürich. Sense of air and
space. They're bundled up against the chill wind.*

Jung I've never met anyone like him. Nothing passes
him by. He understands everything. He's absolutely
extraordinary.

Sabina You know, originally, it was him my mother
wanted me to go to.

Jung Why didn't you?

Sabina My father said he had a scandalous reputation.

Jung reflects for a moment.

Jung I suppose Freud is what's meant by a great man.
I've never met one before. I shall have to be extremely
careful.

Sabina What do you mean?

Jung He's so persuasive, he's so convincing, he makes
you feel you should abandon your own ideas and simply
follow in his wake. I was in Vienna three days, and on
the last day he held his usual weekly meeting. His
followers are all deeply unimpressive: a crowd of
Bohemians and degenerates just picking up the crumbs
from his table.

Sabina Perhaps he's reached the stage where obedience is
more important to him than originality.

Jung Perhaps. I tried to tackle him about his obsession
with sexuality, his insistence on interpreting every
symptom in sexual terms, but he's completely inflexible.

Sabina In my case, of course, he'd have been right.

Jung Yes, as you would expect him to be in many cases, possibly even the majority of cases. (*He shakes his head, troubled.*) But there must be more than one hinge into the universe. (*He broods for a moment, then decides to change the subject.*) I've been reading this new paper by Riklin.

Sabina I like him, he's very sensitive.

Jung frowns, displeased.

Jung He's horribly ambitious, he's an intriguer. And he doesn't know how to develop his ideas, he runs out of steam, gets woolly and speculative. But, yes, he is sensitive.

Sabina suppresses a smile.

Sabina His paper, what's it deal with?

Jung Fairy stories: the symbolic dimensions of myth. For example, he looks at the story of the Frog Prince. He suggests, and of course once it's pointed out, it's obvious, that the underlying meaning of the story is the virgin's fear of sex.

Sabina Ah, yes . . .

Jung Where something ugly and threatening is transformed, through the virgin's daring, into a lifetime of happiness and fulfilment.

Sabina Freud will approve.

Jung I suppose so.

Sabina Although I'd say his interpretation shows a great deal of faith, perhaps too much, in the skill and unselfishness of princes.

Jung You're right.

Not for the first time he's surprised and impressed by her; he looks at her, as she stares out across the lake.

Sabina I look for my ideal in a different myth.

Jung What's that?

Sabina Do you like Wagner?

Jung seems momentarily taken aback.

Jung The music, yes. The man, no.

Sabina The myth of Siegfried: the idea that something pure and heroic can come from a sin, even a sin as dark as incest; the idea that something so perfect can perhaps only be a product of sin.

Jung This is very strange.

Sabina What?

Jung I think I've told you before I don't believe in coincidence, I believe nothing happens by accident, these things have a significance, if only we can penetrate it: the fact is, I'm in the middle of writing something about Wagner and the Siegfried myth.

They look at each other for a moment, their minds racing.

Sabina Are you really?

Jung I assure you.

Sabina Which is your favourite of the operas?

Jung *Das Rheingold.*

Sabina Yes. That's right. Me too. (*Her eyes are shining with excitement.*)

Jung Perhaps we might go sometimes? My wife has never been interested.

Sabina I'd love to.

Jung Freud is sending me a new patient: Otto Gross. Apparently he's a brilliant analyst, although he seems to all intents and purposes to be insane.

Sabina looks up at him, hesitant: then decides to take the plunge.

Sabina Can I ask you something?

Jung Of course.

Sabina Do you think there's any possibility I could ever be a psychiatrist?

Jung turns to look down at her and contemplates her eager expression.

Jung I know you could. I hear nothing but good reports on your work at the University. You're exactly the kind of person we need.

Sabina Insane, you mean?

Jung frowns; then, as he realises she's joking, his expression lightens.

Jung Yes; we sane doctors have serious limitations.

SCENE TWELVE

Jung's office at the Burghölzli: where Otto Gross, a tall, thin, fair, bearded man of thirty with piercing blue eyes and a shabby but elegant suit, leans back comfortably in his armchair, smoking and spraying ash as he gesticulates, his manner relaxed and amused, by contrast to Jung, who sits behind his desk, somewhat constrained and anxious, his manner unusually tentative.

Jung So you do still feel threatened by your father?

Gross Anyone with any sense feels threatened by my father. He's extremely threatening. You know him, of course, as an eminent criminologist, the man who virtually invented a whole new science: footprints, fingerprints, bloodstains, semen samples; and I must tell you that all that scientific paraphernalia is in the pursuit of one very simple aim: to put every single person he disapproves of in jail. You don't have to be a criminal: in fact he wrote a pamphlet about degenerates, explaining that anarchists, tramps, homosexuals, gypsies and perverts – people like me – were far more dangerous than honest criminals and should forthwith be deported to South West Africa. So, in my view, if you didn't feel threatened by him, you'd need your head examined.

Jung You don't think his wish to have you hospitalised arises from a concern for your welfare?

Gross Listen: what does any normal old patriarch want in the twilight of his life? Grandchildren, grandsons, am I right? And yet, last summer, when I presented him with not one, but two little Grosses, one by my wife, one by one of my most respectable mistresses, and we called them both Peter, so he wouldn't get confused, was he grateful? And now there's another one on the way, admittedly by some woman I hardly know, he's apoplectic; and all he wants is to get me banged away in some institution. You got any children?

Jung Two girls.

Gross Same mother?

Jung Yes.

Gross Ah.

Pause. Jung fiddles with his pipe.

Jung I take it, then, you're not a believer in monogamy?

Gross For a neurotic like myself, I can't possibly imagine a more stressful concept.

Jung And you don't find it necessary or desirable to exercise some restraint, as a contribution, say, to the smooth functioning of civilisation?

Gross What, and make myself ill?

Jung I should have thought that some form of sexual repression would have to be exercised in any rational society.

Gross No wonder the hospitals are bulging at the seams. (*He reaches into one of his waistcoat pockets, fetches something out and pops it into his mouth. Then he beams at Jung.*) You are going to help me cut down on this stuff?

Jung I'll do my best.

Gross Good, because it's doing my head in. (*He leans forward, his manner suddenly conspiratorial.*) Tell me, do you find, as I do, there's no better way to enhance your popularity with your patients than to tell them whatever it is they most want to hear?

Jung Does it matter whether we're popular with them or not?

Gross Well, I don't know; suppose you want to fuck them?

Jung looks across at Gross, not certain if he's joking or not; perhaps he isn't, since he now adds something, speaking with the utmost seriousness.

I know very little, but if there's one thing I've learned in my short life, it's this: never repress anything!

SCENE THIRTEEN

A box in the Zürich Opera House: Jung and Sabina sit hand in hand, as the love duet between Siegmund and Sieglinde at the end of the first act of Die Walküre *reaches its ecstatic climax and gives way to a crescendo of mighty chords. There's a burst of applause, the lights come up and Sabina abruptly pulls her hand away. Then she turns to look at Jung for a moment, clearly still strongly affected by the music.*

Sabina When I was working on Siegfried and having that series of dreams about having his baby, your theory was that it was part of the transference and that what it meant was that I wanted to have a child by you.

Jung Yes.

Sabina I resisted your interpretation and got very angry with you: so angry that I should have understood that you were obviously right.

Jung nods almost imperceptibly; he's waiting to see where this is going.

I've been trying to analyse why I continue to feel that way.

Jung And what have you concluded?

Sabina No conclusions, just some thoughts: arising from the idea I take from this opera, that perfection can only be arrived at through what is conventionally thought of as sin. If there's any truth in that, it must surely have to do with the energy created by the friction of opposites; not simply that you're the doctor and I'm the patient, but that you're Swiss and I'm Russian; I'm Jewish and you're Aryan; and other darker differences.

Jung Darker?

Sabina If I'm right, only the clash of destructive forces can create something new. (*Silence. She reaches out to take back his hand.*) When my parents brought me to you, I was very ill; and my illness was sexual. And whatever reservations you may have about Professor Freud's ideas, it's clear this subject I'm studying is entirely grounded in sexuality. So naturally I'm becoming more and more acutely aware of the fact that I have no sexual experience.

Jung Law students are not normally expected to rob banks.

Sabina That's different, as you well know.

They smile at each other; then, impulsively, Sabina leans across, puts her hand round the back of Jung's neck and kisses him on the lips. The kiss lasts some while; then they break away from each other.

Jung It's generally thought to be the man who should take the initiative.

Sabina Don't you think there's something male in every woman? And something female in every man? Or should be?

Jung Maybe. I expect you're right. Yes. You must be.

He considers this for a moment, lost in thought. Sabina moves her chair back, watches him for a while.

Sabina How's your new patient?

Jung Astonishing. I'm spending so much time on him, I'm afraid I'm neglecting some of my other patients.

Sabina What's he like?

Jung Someone in Salzburg once described him as the closest thing you'll ever see to the Romantic notion of a genius.

Sabina Is that how he strikes you?

Jung Well, he's immensely seductive, quite sure he's right and obsessionally neurotic. Pretty dangerous, in fact.

Sabina Does that mean you doubt your power to convince him?

Jung Worse than that: what I'm afraid of is his power to convince me. On the subject of monogamy, for example. Why should we put so much frantic effort into suppressing our most basic natural instincts?

Sabina looks at him for a moment with calculating candour.

Sabina I don't know: you tell me.

Again, they lock eyes; and again, it's Sabina who changes the subject.

How's your new house?

Jung What?

Sabina Your new house, how's it coming along?

Jung Oh, it'll be at least a year before it's ready. But it's away from the city and on the lake and it should be quiet, it should be a wonderful place to work. It's something my wife wanted to do for me. And anyway, soon we'll have run out of space. She's pregnant again.

Sabina winces, unable to conceal her dismay.

Sabina Is she?

Jung This time, she's sure it's a boy.

Sabina No.

Jung What do you mean, no?

Sabina I'm the one to give you a son.

Jung's office at the Burghölzli: Otto Gross looks across the desk at Jung, his eyes sparkling with mischief and provocation.

Gross I can't understand what you're waiting for. Just take her to some secluded spot and thrash her to within an inch of her life: that's clearly what she wants. How can you deny her such a simple pleasure?

Jung Pleasure is never simple, as I'm sure you know.

Gross It is, of course it is, until we decide to complicate it. The tragedy of childhood is the moment we understand we can never have everything we want; the tragedy of adulthood is the moment we decide not to take everything we can have: what my father calls maturity, what I call surrender.

Jung Surrender, for me, would be to give in to these urges.

Gross Then surrender: doesn't matter what you call it as long as you don't let the experience escape. That's my prescription.

Jung I'm supposed to be treating you.

Gross Yes, and it's been most effective. I'm down to three grammes of opium a day.

Jung That's excellent progress.

Gross Yes. (*He contemplates Jung through narrowed eyes.*) So are you seriously telling me you've never slept with any of your patients?

Jung Of course I haven't: one has to steer through the temptations of transference and counter-transference, that's an essential stage of the process.

Gross When transference occurs, when the patient becomes fixated on me, I explain to her that this is merely a symbol of her wretched monogamous habits: I show her that it's fine to want to sleep with me, but only if, at the same time, she acknowledges to herself that she wants to sleep with a great many other people.

Jung Suppose she doesn't?

Gross Then it's my job to convince her that that's part of the illness.

Silence. Jung shakes his head, troubled.

This is what people are like. And if we don't tell them the truth, who will?

Jung has decided to approach from another direction.

Jung You agree with Freud, then? You think all neurosis is of exclusively sexual origin?

Gross Well, I think Freud's obsession with sex probably has a great deal to do with the fact that he never gets any, don't you?

Jung can't help smiling.

Jung I suppose it's possible.

Gross In those circumstances, it's bound to prey on your mind; even at his age.

Jung You could be right.

Gross It seems to me a measure of the true perversity of the human race that one of its few reliably pleasurable experiences should be the subject of so much hysteria and repression. The story of our life is essentially the story of our sexuality, isn't it? And what my father calls immorality is surely the only possible healthy state for any neurotic. To repress yourself must be to condemn

44

yourself to realise no more than a fragment of your full psychic potential.

Jung is following him, fascinated but still dubious.

Jung But not to repress yourself is to unleash all kinds of dangerous and destructive forces.

Gross One of the reasons I love Nietzsche, although I could never bring myself to approve of his moustache, was his firm belief that the superior being, namely oneself, was above and beyond laws and conventions. Our job is to make our patients capable of freedom.

Jung I've heard it said you helped one of your patients to kill herself.

Gross looks evenly across at him, untroubled.

Gross She was resolutely suicidal. I just explained how she could do it without botching it. Then I asked her if she didn't prefer the idea of becoming my lover. She said she didn't see why the one should preclude the other. She opted for both.

Jung That can't be what we want for our patients.

Gross Freedom is freedom. (*He sits up, suddenly serious.*) Life being what it is, the more sensitive you are, the sicker you'll become. So I say, whenever you see an oasis, you must always remember to drink.

He seems about to say something else, but at this point, quite suddenly, a stream of dark blood begins to flow from one nostril. He dabs at himself, bemused, then looks down at the blood on his fingertips. Jung masters his shock and hands him a white handkerchief, which he uses to clean up, although for the moment the blood continues to flow. Eventually, he answers the question in Jung's eyes.

45

I gave up the opium, but you can't expect me to give up the cocaine as well.

Jung If this is the result, I think you must: I don't see how you can go on.

Gross is looking up at him now, wiping the blood away, his expression suddenly defiant.

Gross I'll use the other fucking nostril.

SCENE FIFTEEN

Sabina's austere attic room, with its mansard ceiling and narrow single bed, at 7, Schönleinstrasse in Zürich. Jung and Sabina are on the floor, wrapped in a blanket, Jung propped up against the desk in the open window, through which floods a cascade of moonlight. The bed is open and there's blood on the sheets. There's silence, except for distant sounds of the city, odd voices, the rattle of trams. Eventually, Sabina reaches up to stroke Jung's cheek; he smiles down at her, then looks away, his expression haunted.

Jung If I say something, will you promise not to take it the wrong way?

Sabina What?

Jung Don't you think we ought to stop now?

Sabina looks up at him, appalled.

Jung I'm married: obviously I'm being deceitful. Is it right for us to perpetuate this deceit, over and over again?

Sabina Do you want to stop?

Jung Of course I don't. I'm in love with you.

He leans down and kisses her passionately. Then she draws back, looks up at him and speaks very quietly.

Sabina When you make love to your wife, how is it?

Jung What do you mean?

Sabina Describe it to me.

Jung If you live under the same roof with someone, no matter how much you love them, it's habit, you know, the excitement, the intoxication is bound to wear off. It's always . . . very tender.

Sabina Then this is another thing. Another thing in another country. With me, I want you to be . . . ferocious. I want you to punish me.

Jung continues to look down at her, his expression uncertain.

There's a Russian poem keeps going round my head, Lermontov, I think, about a prisoner who finally achieves some happiness when he succeeds in releasing a bird from its cage.

Jung Why do you think this is preoccupying you?

Sabina I think it means that when I'm a doctor, I want more than anything else to give people back their freedom by curing them, the way you gave me mine.

Jung And you've given me mine, because this is what freedom is: no constraints, no chains, where love isn't a means to an end, it's an end in itself.

Sabina So this is love, this is what love is?

Jung What else could it be, this beauty, this absolute physical ease? Unless it's something even more important.

Sabina More important than love?

Jung Maybe.

Sabina What could that be?

Jung strokes her shoulder for a moment, thinking.

Jung The future?

Sabina shakes her head, disturbed.

Sabina No. (*She looks up at him.*) I don't like to think about the future.

Jung Why not?

Sabina looks away, doesn't answer.

SCENE SIXTEEN

Wasteland. Heat. A complete change of atmosphere. Enough indications to let us know we are in Russia, Rostov-on-Don, in fact, in the summer of 1942. At first, the stage is empty; then a small child, a girl, perhaps about six, wanders into view, intent on something, maybe following the flight of a butterfly. Just offstage, there's the sense of a shuffling, uncomfortable crowd. Then a tall, uniformed S.S. Officer strides on, shouting at the little girl.

Officer Get back!

The girl glances at him, then decides to ignore him and pursue her goal. He steps after her, raising a meaty hand to strike her; but he's stopped by a sudden cry offstage.

Sabina (*offstage*) Stop!

Sabina appears; she's in her fifties now, shabby and unkempt, but surprisingly unchanged. The S.S. Officer is looking at her in amazement. She speaks with calm authority.

Don't you know that to strike a child is the worst possible thing you can do?

Officer Is that so? And where did you learn such good German?

Sabina I studied in Munich. I'm a doctor.

Officer Well, Dr Jew, see if you can cure this.

He takes his pistol out of its holster and shoots her.

Interval.

Act Two

Sabina's room: it's daytime, but the curtains are closed. Sabina is in bed, watching unhappily as Jung finishes dressing. The heavy silence lasts. Finally, his tie knotted and his jacket on, Jung reaches for a chair and sits down not far away from her, his expression grave.

Jung When I fall in love, one of my first instincts is to feel sorry for the woman involved, because I know, whatever she may imagine when the affair starts, what she really wants is something permanent, the everlasting peace of the double bed, something *resolved*. Whereas what I'm looking for is something different every time, something wild, untrammelled, in and of the moment.

Sabina But so am I.

Jung Then I'm confused, I feel trapped, I've trapped myself into feeling divided and . . . guilty.

Sabina I don't want you to feel guilty, I've never wanted anything like that.

Jung I don't see how we can go on.

He rises unsteadily to his feet; Sabina springs out of bed and throws her arms around him.

Sabina You mustn't say that.

Jung I have some kind of illness. Try to remember the love and patience I showed towards you when you were ill. That's what I need from you now.

Sabina Of course. You have it. Always. But please don't go.

50

He looks down at her trembling body.

Jung I must. I have to. (*He breaks away from her, gathers up his hat and coat and hurries out of the room.*)

SCENE TWO

The delivery room at the Burghölzli: it's moments after the birth of Jung's son, Franz, and the baby is being handed to Emma by a young Nurse. Emma looks exhausted but happy; Jung beams down at her, exhilarated and proud.

Emma I knew it was a boy this time, I told you, he felt different.

Jung I believed you.

Emma tucks the baby into the cradle of her arm, reaching for Jung with her other hand. The Nurse leaves the room.

Emma When you get back to the house, the boat should be there.

Jung Boat?

Emma The boat with red sails: I know you've always wanted it. It should be tied up at the jetty by now.

Jung Thank you. (*He takes her in his arms and kisses her.*) Thank you for everything. Our son, our beautiful house . . .

Emma You're a good man. You deserve everything good.

Jung No.

Emma nods, contradicting him.

Emma Will you come back to us now?

Jung What do you mean?

Emma Surely you didn't think we'd let you go without putting up a fight?

Concealing his amazement, Jung reaches out to move aside an unruly lock of hair and kisses Emma reverently on the forehead.

SCENE THREE

Jung's office at the Burghölzli. He's sitting, very tense, behind his desk, waiting. He checks the clock on his desk. He gets up and paces for a while. He's just sat down again, when there's a knock at the door.

Jung Come in.

Sabina surges into the room.

Sabina Why are you doing this?

Jung Please sit down.

Sabina How could you treat me this way?

Jung Sit down!

There's a tense silence: then she sits down some way away from the desk.

I tried to explain the situation to your mother.

Sabina I don't know how you dared say those things to her.

Jung She came to me waving some anonymous letter, demanding to know if it was true. I told her obviously it was a confidential matter, but that even if it were true, the position would not be quite as she imagined, since you were no longer my patient.

Sabina Of course I'm your patient!

Jung Technically not, not since I stopped charging you.

Sabina That's what she said; I told her I didn't believe her, and she told me you said your fee was ten francs a consultation.

Jung I was trying to point out to her that I would take you back as a patient, if that was what was required, but that I could only undertake to see you inside this office, on an entirely formal basis.

Sabina How could you be so cold and offhand?

Jung I was trying to make her understand the distinction between a patient and a friend.

Silence. Jung makes a huge effort to control himself.

Listen, I've made a stupid mistake.

Sabina Is that what it was?

Jung I broke one of the elementary rules of my profession. I'm your doctor: and I believe I did you some good. I can't forgive myself for overstepping the mark: I should have known that if I let go and gave you what you wanted, you wouldn't be able to help wanting more.

Sabina I don't want more, I never wanted more, I never asked for more.

Jung You didn't have to ask.

Sabina Even if you're right, which I dispute, you think this is a proper way to behave towards me? Refusing to speak to me except in your office?

Jung I'm your physician: from now on, that's all I can be.

Silence. Finally, Sabina looks up at him.

Sabina Don't you love me any more?

Jung Only as your physician.

Sabina You think I'm going to stand for this?

Jung What choice do you have?

Moving with tremendous speed, Sabina's on her feet and round the desk, where she deals him a staggering open-handed blow to the face. The assault continues and Jung is forced to struggle to his feet under a rain of blows, until he's able to grip her wrists. He looms over her, still stunned by the violence of her attack.

You have to understand: I'm your physician!

She's glaring fiercely at him; as soon as he releases her wrists, once again moving like lightning, she grabs a paper-knife from the desk and lunges at him.

Sabina Then heal thyself!

She's opened a gash in his cheek: and as he puts up an astonished hand to feel the blood which is starting to well, she goes for him again. This time, he's able to grasp her wrist and, after a short, vicious struggle, disarms her. She takes a couple of steps back, still shaking with fury. Then she reaches into her bag, pulls out a ten-franc note and slaps it onto his cheek, where it adheres.

And there's your ten francs!

She rushes from the room, leaving Jung standing amazed, reaching up to peel the banknote from his bloody cheek.

SCENE FOUR

Freud's study in his apartment in Vienna: two years on from his first meeting with Jung, who this time seems considerably less comfortable, the gash from Sabina's attack still visible on his cheek. The full ashtray is an indication of how long the discussion has been going; and in the course of the scene, both men indulge in considerable amounts of cigar and pipe work. It's the middle of the night.

Freud It's very confusing: first I hear this rumour that you've taken a mistress in Zürich.

Jung What? (*He's very shocked.*)

Freud Yes, one of your patients, they say.

Jung Who says?

Freud Muthmann: he tells me the woman is boasting all over town.

Jung It's absolutely untrue.

Freud I was sure of it. But then I get a curious letter from this person who says she wants to come and see me in Vienna on a matter of great interest to both of us . . .

He hands a letter to Jung, who runs his eye over it, trying extremely hard to conceal his emotions.

Jung Oh, this is from Spielrein: you remember, the Russian, my first psychoanalytic case.

Freud Yes, of course: it was she, in some sense, who brought us together.

Jung That's right: I've always been fond of her and grateful to her for that reason. I let her become a friend.

Freud Yes?

Jung But eventually I realised she was systematically planning my seduction.

Freud And?

Jung I broke with her: now, I suppose, she's plotting her revenge.

Freud shakes his head, amusement in his eyes.

Freud These women: the way they try to seduce us, the way they use every conceivable psychic wile. It's one of nature's most dramatic spectacles.

Jung And, you know, I've never shown such friendship to any other patient. (*He shakes his head, reflecting.*) Your famous saying is carved in block letters on my heart.

Freud Which one?

Jung When you said: 'Whatever you do, give up any idea of trying to cure them.'

Freud Look at it this way: these painful experiences in life are in fact necessary and inevitable. Without them, how would we know life?

Jung You're right, of course. (*He glances at Freud, trying to gauge if the moment is right for his big piece of news; and decides to go ahead.*) I've resigned from the hospital.

Freud I had heard something of the sort.

Jung Oh. (*He's very surprised and deflated.*)

Freud Only, to tell you the truth, what I had heard was that you had been dismissed.

Jung No: absolutely not. The pretext was that the new lectureship in mental hygiene, which should have been offered automatically to the Assistant Director, was actually offered to Riklin, on the grounds that his little book on fairy stories had caused such a stir. But the real reason is that I want to practise privately at home, as you do, and not have my research time eaten into with hospital administration. And, of course, there's our *Yearbook* to think of.

Freud Naturally.

Jung No, no, the Herr Direktor was most put out. He kept asking me the *real* reason for my resignation. Finally, I said, well, Herr Direktor, after eight years of your regime, I need a drink.

He laughs nervously and Freud smiles politely, clearly not believing a word of it.

I told him I'd stay three months, until he could find someone.

Freud Well, I'm sure you've made the right decision.

Silence. Jung still seems anxious.

Jung What was the second thing?

Freud I beg your pardon?

Jung You said, first you'd heard a rumour . . .

Freud Oh. Oh, yes. Secondly, I wanted to take you up on one or two phrases in your recent letters I've found a bit troubling.

Jung frowns, perplexed, as Freud reaches for more sheets of paper from his desk.

Here, this is just a straw in the wind, this is when you wrote to me about Pfister. You say: 'Strangely enough, I like his mixture of medicine and theology.'

Jung Yes.

Freud Not, in my opinion, at all a good mixture.

Jung I see.

Freud And then you go to see Häberlin . . . (*He reaches for a different letter.*) And here you say: 'I particularly approve of his mystical streak, a guarantee of a more than ordinary profundity.'

Jung Well, I . . .

Freud I don't want you to think I have a closed mind . . .

Jung Of course not.

Freud I've no objection to people researching into thought transference or parapsychology to their hearts' content. But I would want to make the point that our own field is so embattled, it can only be dangerous to stray into any kind of mysticism. Don't you see? We have to stay within the most rigorously scientific confines . . .

He breaks off, noticing that Jung is resting his hand on his stomach, with an increasingly pained expression.

Are you all right?

Jung Yes; but I can't agree with you. Why should we draw some arbitrary line and close off whole areas of investigation?

Freud Precisely because the world is full of enemies, looking for any way they can devise to discredit us. And the minute they see us abandon the firm ground of the sexual theory to wallow in the black mud of superstition, they'll pounce. Perhaps you don't understand just how precarious our position is. As far as I'm concerned, even to raise these subjects would be professional suicide; you really must . . .

Again he breaks off, this time because the wood in his bookcase has cracked, with a report like a gun, so loud it causes Freud to duck involuntarily.

What in God's name was that?

Jung I knew that was going to happen.

Freud What?

Jung I felt something like that was going to happen. I had a kind of burning in my stomach.

Freud What are you talking about? It's the heating, the wood in the bookcase just cracked, that's all.

Jung No, it's what's known as a catalytic exteriorisation phenomenon.

Freud A what?

Jung A catalytic exteriorisation phenomenon.

Freud Don't be ridiculous.

Jung It started with this feeling: as if my diaphragm was glowing red-hot . . .

Freud I know it's late, but you really shouldn't . . .

Jung And another thing: it's going to happen again.

Freud What?

Jung In a minute, it's going to happen again.

Freud This is exactly the kind of thing I'm talking about: my dear young friend, you must promise me to . . .

But he's interrupted by another loud report from the bookshelf. He looks up at it, for once entirely at a loss for words.

Jung You see.

Freud That's just . . . you really can't . . .

Jung There's so much more, so many mysteries, so much further to go.

Freud Please. We can't be too careful. We cannot afford to wander into these speculative areas, telepathy, singing bookcases, fairies at the bottom of the garden. Remember Otto Gross.

Jung What's become of him?

Freud You haven't seen him?

Jung Not since he seduced the nurse, took her into town with him and sent me the hotel bill. Where is he?

Freud Skulking around Munich.

Jung He's a remarkable man.

Freud No; he's an addict. He can only end one way: by doing great harm to our movement.

Jung No, the harm will be to himself; if you have no notion of reality, how can you recognise it when it comes towards you with a knife in its hand?

Freud It looks as if something's come towards you with a knife in its hand.

Jung's hand reaches automatically to his cheek.

Jung Shaving accident.

Freud How disappointing: I thought at least you'd been involved in a duel. Not inappropriate for a crown prince.

Jung What do you mean?

Freud Don't you realise, with Gross in irrevocable decline, you are now the undisputed dauphin. And when the *Yearbook* comes out, with your name on the masthead, your position will be clear to everyone.

Jung What position?

Freud My son and heir.

Silence. Jung frowns.

Jung I'm not sure I deserve . . .

Freud Don't say another word. I shall tell them all about you in America, rest assured.

Jung When do you leave?

Freud August. (*He beams complacently at Jung.*) As to the matter of Miss Spielrein, I shall write and tell her I know you're incapable of shabby behaviour, and I suggest she recall the positive feelings you aroused in her, rather than dwell on the destructive resentments she may now be experiencing. And naturally I shall refuse to see her.

Jung looks enormously relieved.

Jung I knew if you really thought of me as your son and heir, you wouldn't believe I'd be stupid enough to get emotionally involved with a patient.

SCENE FIVE

Jung's office at the Burghölzli: the desk is clear and a number of cardboard boxes bear witness to his imminent departure. Jung is checking the drawers, when he's surprised by a light tap at the door. The scar on his cheek has disappeared.

Jung Yes?

He's surprised to see Sabina slip into the room. She stands looking at him; and it's a while before he's sufficiently composed to speak.

What is it?

Sabina I heard you were leaving the hospital.

Jung As you see.

Sabina And people are saying it's because of the scandal I caused.

Jung Well, as you know, I'd been planning to leave anyway.

Sabina I'm sorry if I . . . precipitated it.

Jung You've always been . . . something of a catalyst.

Their initial defensiveness is beginning to soften.

Sabina I've had a letter from Professor Freud.

Jung Oh, yes?

Sabina The thing that shone through most clearly was how much he loves you. I was very touched by it.

Jung Well, that's . . . (*He breaks off, his pleasure at this news not altogether unmixed.*)

Sabina But what was also clear is that you denied everything. Didn't you? You let him think I was a fantasist or a liar.

Jung I didn't necessarily think it was any of his business.

Sabina I've come to ask you to tell him the truth.

Jung What?

Sabina I want you to write and tell him everything: including what you said to my mother.

Jung is clearly horrified by this suggestion. He sits down abruptly.

And tell him I want him to write to me again, to confirm that you've told him everything.

Jung Are you blackmailing me?

Sabina No: I'm asking you to tell the truth.

Jung Why is this so important to you?

Sabina Because now you're not available to me any more, I need someone else. I want him to take me as his patient.

Jung But does it have to be him?

Sabina It has to be him.

Jung shakes his head, tormented at the thought.

You don't feel the same way about him, do you?

Jung I'm disappointed by his rigid insistence that nothing can possibly exist unless some puny and transitory intelligence has become aware of it.

Sabina Nevertheless, will you write to him?

Jung looks away, doesn't answer.

I could have damaged you, you know, far worse than I did. I chose not to.

Jung All right, I'll do it.

Sabina Thank you. It means everything to me.

Jung moves over to look out of the window.

Jung Are you going somewhere for the summer?

Sabina Berlin, with my parents.

Jung But you are going to come back here to the University? And qualify?

Sabina Of course.

Jung I'm going to America. With Freud, although he doesn't yet know it. He's been boasting about this trip all year. And last week, they invited me.

Sabina Are you excited?

Jung What's slightly embarrassing is that Emma insisted on reserving me a first-class stateroom. And I'm afraid Freud may be travelling second class.

Sabina All the same, it is exciting, isn't it?

Jung Yes; the visit is potentially very important for the whole movement.

Sabina I'm sure. Well: goodbye.

Jung turns back from the window, surprised; but she's already on her way out of the room.

SCENE SIX

The deck of the S.S. George Washington, mid-Atlantic: it's deserted, perhaps because of the penetrating chill of the ghostly Atlantic fog, except for the towering figure of Jung, who's shepherding the frail person of Freud, wrapped in heavy overcoat and plaid blanket.

Jung I was on the Swiss-Austrian border, somewhere in the mountains, at dusk. There was a long wait, because everybody's baggage was being searched. At a certain point, I noticed a decrepit customs official, wearing the old royal and imperial uniform. I was watching him walking up and down, his melancholy and disgruntled expression, when someone said to me: 'He isn't really there, you know, he's a ghost, who still hasn't found out how to die properly.'

Freud Is that it? The whole dream?

Jung All I can remember.

Freud Did you say the Swiss-Austrian border?

Jung Yes.

Freud It must have something to do with us.

Jung You think so?

Freud Everything being searched, eh? Perhaps it's an indication that the ideas which used to flow so freely between us are now subject to the most suspicious kind of examination.

Jung You mean the ideas flowing in your direction.

Freud And I'm afraid the odd relic shuffling about in this entirely useless fashion must almost certainly be me.

Jung No, wait a minute . . .

Freud Whom you very mercifully wish could be put out of his misery. A humane death wish.

Jung Perhaps the fact he was unable to die simply indicated the immortality of his ideas.

Freud So you agree it must have been me.

Jung I didn't say that.

Freud Never mind, it's a most entertaining example. (*He stops for a moment, to look out to sea.*)

Jung What about you, do you have a dream to report?

Freud I had a most elaborate dream last night. Particularly rich.

Jung Oh, let's hear it.

Silence. Jung is left staring at Freud's back. Finally, Freud speaks.

Freud I'd love to tell you, but I don't think I should.

Jung Why ever not?

Freud turns to look at him, accompanying his reply with a peculiarly mirthless smile.

Freud I wouldn't want to risk my authority.

Jung is nonplussed by this remark. He can think of no satisfactory response. Oblivious to this, Freud changes the subject.

By the way, did I tell you? I wrote to your Russian girl.

Jung Oh, yes? (*His tone is distant.*)

Freud I apologised to her, and said I was relieved to know the truth, which fully satisfied my neurotic desire to revere women. I said I was impressed by the dignified way she'd coped with a complicated situation.

Jung Yes, I'm very glad I wasn't mistaken about the essential decency of her character; and I'm sorry I was stupid enough to involve you in the matter.

Freud Not at all: all's well that ends well.

Jung Did she . . . ask you to take her on as a patient?

Freud She did, yes.

Silence. Jung fails to prevent himself from asking the next question.

Jung And did you accept?

Freud I said she should come and see me when she's next in Vienna.

For a moment, Jung doesn't know what to say.

Jung I don't know how I could have committed such a disastrous, elementary blunder . . . it's enough to make one doubt one's ambitions.

It's Freud's turn to look quizzically at Jung for a moment.

Freud Do you know, I don't think I've ever been in the least ambitious. I'm probably the only person I know with no ambition whatsoever.

Jung's mouth opens and shuts, too staggered by the preposterousness of Freud's remark to utter a sound. He casts about for some entirely new topic.

Jung Just before we left Bremen, I read a most interesting article about the peat-bog corpses they've recently found in Schleswig-Holstein.

Freud What a very disagreeable topic.

Jung It's evidently a kind of natural mummification that takes place, except that of course the bodies are pressed flat by the weight of the peat.

Freud is beginning to look queasy.

Freud Is that so?

Jung One of the interesting features is that so many of the corpses have died violent deaths, are found with ropes around their necks or even severed heads.

Freud If you persist in talking about corpses, I shall know for certain that you are harbouring a death wish.

Jung smiles, choosing to acknowledge this as a joke, which it clearly isn't.

Jung But they are perfectly preserved, because the humic acid contained in the bog water dissolves the bones, while at the same time tanning the loose skin like a hide . . .

He breaks off: he has to, because Freud has pitched forward in a dead faint. Fortunately, Jung's reflexes are quick enough for him to catch Freud; and he supports him for the few seconds it takes for Freud to regain consciousness.

Are you all right?

Freud Of course I am; what happened?

Jung You fainted.

*Freud seems about to deny this indignantly; but he
thinks better of it.*

Freud I did ask you not to persist with that disgusting
line of conversation.

Jung I'm sorry, I had no idea . . . Look, we'd better get
you back to your cabin. I'll order some beef tea.

Freud Well, it is a little chilly.

Jung I meant to ask, would you like me to wake you
tomorrow morning?

Freud What for?

Jung We're due to dock at dawn. I thought you might
like to watch our approaches to New York harbour from
my stateroom.

Freud Well . . .

Jung You wouldn't want to miss our arrival in America.

Freud I don't know about America. Whenever I think
about it, I can't help feeling there's been some gigantic
mistake.

Jung Oh, no. No! America is the future.

*He tries to help Freud along the deck, but the older
man rather tetchily shakes himself free.*

SCENE SEVEN

The following year, 1910, and Sabina, her hair fashionably restyled, wearing her best dress, waits in Jung's beautifully designed new study at Küsnacht, with its monumental desk and its views of the garden leading down to the lake. But Sabina's dress is torn at the knee and her umbrella, which she's still holding, is bent almost into a C-shape. She's looking out of the window, and so is considerably startled by the arrival of Agathe Jung, a small, pretty six-year-old, who announces her presence by tugging at Sabina's dress.

Agathe What's your name?

Sabina Sabina.

Agathe Sabina. Hello, Sabina. My name's Agathe.

Sabina Hello, Agathe.

Agathe You've torn your dress.

Sabina That's right.

Agathe And your umbrella's broken.

Sabina I had a little accident.

Jung Nothing serious, I hope.

His voice, which slightly precedes his appearance makes Sabina almost jump out of her skin. She pulls herself together determinedly.

Sabina Well, I could see the ferry was about to leave, so I jumped out of the tram before it stopped.

Agathe Did you catch the ferry?

Sabina Well, I did, yes.

Agathe Then it was worth it.

Jung Run along, my dear, I'll see you at lunch.

Agathe Are you staying to lunch?

Jung I don't think she can today.

Agathe Goodbye, Sabina.

Sabina Goodbye, Agathe.

The little girl runs out of the room, leaving the two adults looking intensely constrained. Finally, Jung breaks the silence.

Jung I expect you've heard the expression 'wish-fulfilment'. I've always thought there was an equivalent process called 'fear-fulfilment'. Are you sure that's not what you were doing, jumping from a moving tram?

Sabina It was an accident.

Jung Your friend Professor Freud would have you believe there's no such thing.

Sabina Well, of course. I was nervous: not having seen you for over a year.

Jung Yes, it's strange how one can live in the same city and frequent the same university without ever setting eyes on one another.

Sabina Yes.

Jung Yes, I was nervous too. (*He motions to her to sit down and reaches for a bulky document on his desk.*) Well, now, whose idea was it that you should send me your dissertation?

Sabina The Herr Direktor.

Jung Ah, yes, of course.

Sabina Obviously he thought your comments would be very valuable; but he also kept insisting that this was the kind of material you were looking for for your *Yearbook*.

Jung Well, it is; and it certainly is a most fascinating case you've chosen to investigate. There're some really good things here; I was genuinely delighted to read it, I assure you.

Sabina Good, I'm so glad.

Jung But if we're to consider it for the *Yearbook*, there are a number of gaps which need filling and a few downright mistakes which will have to be dealt with.

Sabina Well, of course.

Jung Would you have a little time to discuss all this?

Sabina Yes. Yes, certainly.

Jung You know when we moved out here, I was afraid it would take years to build up a roster of patients, but I'm afraid we're already under siege. (*He reaches for his diary, begins to consult it.*)

Sabina How's . . . Mrs Jung?

Jung Very well: I don't suppose you'll be amazed to hear she's expecting another addition to the family to arrive next week.

Sabina Oh. Please give her my congratulations.

Jung I will.

Sabina Your house is beautiful.

Jung Thank you. Anyway, as I was saying, I don't see why a little more work shouldn't make your dissertation eminently publishable.

Sabina Do you think we'd be able to work on it together without . . . ?

Jung Oh, yes: that is if you mean what I think you mean. As long as it's all right with you.

Sabina Yes, I'm sure I . . .

She breaks off. They look at each other for a moment.

Jung It's always going to be a risk, seeing one another.

Sabina Yes.

Jung But I believe we have the character to be able to deal with the situation, don't you?

Sabina I hope so.

But it is a dangerous silence which ensues.

I somehow imagined you would have found another admirer by now.

Jung looks away; then back to her.

Jung No. You were the jewel of great price.

Sabina lowers her eyes; then makes a supreme effort.

Sabina How was your trip to America?

Jung A triumph. I've been invited back. On my own.

Sabina Well . . . that is good.

Jung Shall we say this time next Tuesday? And I'll start gently ripping you to shreds.

Sabina You don't have to be too gentle. (*She rises abruptly to her feet.*)

Jung Wait.

She stands there, looking at him, frozen to the spot.

Before you go, I have a few minutes; I did want to ask you something about this. Sit down.

He picks up the dissertation again, as she resumes her seat.

Talk to me about this analogy you make between the death instinct and the sex instinct.

Sabina My starting point was to consider Professor Freud's characterisation of the sexual drive as arising from a simple urge towards pleasure; I wondered, if his assumption was correct, why this urge is so often successfully repressed.

Jung You used to have a theory involving the impulse towards destruction and self-destruction: losing oneself.

Sabina I don't believe that any more; or rather, I tried changing the elements. Suppose we think of sexuality as fusion, losing oneself, as you say, but losing oneself in the other, destroying one's own individuality? Wouldn't the ego, in self-defence, automatically resist and repress that impulse?

Jung You mean, not for social but for selfish reasons?

Sabina Yes, I'm saying that perhaps true sexuality demands the destruction of the ego.

Jung In other words, the opposite of what Freud proposes?

Sabina In a way.

Jung thinks about this for a moment. He rises to his feet, in the grip of considerable intellectual excitement.

Jung But . . . that implies that the repressive mechanism is not manufactured within the individual himself, but arises from some kind of . . . inborn communal instinct.

Sabina That's right.

Jung Hm. (*He's standing at the window now, his eyes bright as he examines the many implications of Sabina's proposal. After a time, he turns his gaze on her.*) Every time I see you, it becomes easier to understand why I fell in love with you.

Sabina Does it?

> *There's a silence, during which he moves round, until he's standing above her. She looks calmly up at him.*

Sabina It would mean so much to me if we could be friends again.

Jung Yes.

Sabina Isn't this kind of dispassionate friendship even more beautiful than what we had before?

> *Jung hesitates for a long time; then he answers, hoarsely.*

Jung No.

> *He drops to his knees and takes her in his arms. There's the briefest moment of resistance; then she succumbs and they're lost in a profound embrace.*

SCENE EIGHT

Sabina's room: it's late afternoon and she lies in Jung's arms on her narrow bed. He seems peaceful, satiated.

Jung I want you to tell me you haven't given a thought to your examinations all afternoon.

Sabina It wouldn't quite be true. They are next week.

Jung You're going to do very very well.

Sabina I don't think so.

Jung Of course you are. Have you decided what you want to do afterwards? Will you stay on at the University?

Sabina moves her head to look gravely at Jung.

Sabina No. I'm going to leave Zürich.

Jung Oh. Are you sure?

Sabina I have to.

Jung looks at her; he's been dreading this.

Jung Why?

Sabina You know why.

Jung I thought maybe we could . . .

Sabina What? Keep meeting like this?

Jung doesn't answer.

You're never going to leave your wife, are you? No; and I don't want you to. Why should she suffer? I certainly have nothing against her. If you love her, I'm sure she must be a good person.

Jung But it's not like us: she doesn't know what I'm going to say before I say it, the way you do. She can't be a partner in my work.

Sabina You knew that very well when you married her. That may even be why you married her.

Silence, broken by a deep sigh from Jung.

Jung It's true: I'm nothing but a philistine Swiss bourgeois. A complacent coward. I wish I could break away and leave everything and disappear with you and then . . . comes the voice of the philistine.

75

Sabina If you were free, do you think you would want to marry me?

Jung Of course; of course I would.

Sabina Well, I want to be free. I must be free. That's why I have to leave.

Jung Where will you go?

Sabina I don't know. Vienna, maybe.

Jung Please don't go there.

Sabina I must go wherever I need to go to feel free.

Abruptly, Jung bursts into tears, burying his face in her breast.

Jung Don't.

She looks down at his large head and heaving shoulders with infinite sadness, but, as she reaches out to stroke his hair, she's dry-eyed and determined-looking.

SCENE NINE

Freud's study: but this time it's Sabina who sits with him, comfortable in the mellow lamplight. He's lighting his cigar and contemplating her benevolently across his desk. It's the summer of 1912.

Freud I assure you, it was a most impressive address; although it was an unpleasant shock, almost at the end, when you suddenly introduced the name of Christ.

Sabina I wasn't making any sort of religious point. I was drawing an analogy between the myth of Christ and the myth of Siegfried.

Freud All the same, in my view, it's a name to be avoided; it always starts me thinking about Swiss Protestantism.

76

He pauses, waiting to see if Sabina rises to the bait; she doesn't.

But no, the evening was a resounding success, and led to one of the most stimulating discussions we've ever had at the Psychoanalytic Society. Do you really think the sexual drive . . . (*He breaks off briefly to consult his notes.*) . . . is a 'demonic and destructive force'?

Sabina Yes, at the same time as being a creative force, in the sense that it can produce, out of the destruction of two individualities, a new being. But the individual always has to overcome a resistance because of the self-annihilating nature of the sexual act.

Freud Well, I've been hostile to the idea for some reason, but the more I think about it, the more obvious it becomes, but there must be some kind of indissoluble link between sex and death. I don't feel the relationship between the two is quite as you've portrayed it, but I'm most grateful to you for animating the subject in such a stimulating way.

Sabina Are you completely opposed to any kind of religious dimension in our field?

Freud Not in principle: but I will say that more crimes have been committed in the name of religion than for any other cause. All the same, in general, I don't care if a man believes in Rama, Marx or Aphrodite, as long as he keeps it out of the consulting room.

Sabina Is that what's at the basis of your dispute with Dr Jung?

Freud I have no dispute with Dr Jung. I was simply mistaken about him. I thought he was going to be able to carry our work forward after I was gone; but I didn't know him well enough. I didn't bargain for all that second-rate mysticism and self-aggrandising shamanism. I didn't realise he could be so brutal and sanctimonious.

Sabina What he's trying to do is find some way forward, so that we don't just have to tell our patients, this is why you are the way you are; he wants to be able to say, we can show you what you might expect to become.

Freud Playing God, in other words. We have no right to do that. The world is as it is: understanding and accepting that is the way to psychic health. What good can we do if our aim is simply to replace one delusion with another?

Sabina Well, I agree with you.

Freud Yes; I couldn't help noticing that in the crucial areas of dispute between Dr Jung and myself, you undoubtedly favour me.

Sabina I thought you had no dispute with him.

Freud smiles, acknowledging he's been caught out. Then, his brow furrows.

Freud You still love him, don't you?

Sabina Yes, but that's not why I'm pleading his cause. I just feel that if the two of you don't find a way to co-exist, it will hold back the progress of psychoanalysis, perhaps indefinitely.

Freud If you still love him, it's because you haven't yet understood the hatred he deserves. I believe he's quite capable of destroying all the good work of the last twenty years and putting nothing of value in its place. However, since you do love him, I'll restrain myself.

Sabina Is there no way to avert a total rupture?

Freud Of course, correct scientific relations will be maintained. And I shall no doubt be seeing him at the editorial meeting in Munich in November, and I shall be perfectly civil and see if there isn't some way of rekindling the ashes. But, to tell you the truth, what finished him for me was all that business about you, the lies, the ruthless behaviour. I was very shocked on your behalf.

Sabina I know he loved me.

Freud All the more reason to behave better, wouldn't you say? And I'm afraid your idea of a mystical union with a blond Siegfried was inevitably doomed. Put not your trust in Aryans. We're Jews, my dear Miss Spielrein; and Jews we will always be.

She's looking at him, surprised by the sudden intensity in his voice. Aware of this, he takes another puff of his cigar and changes his tone.

Now: the real reason I invited you here was to ask if you'd be prepared to take on one or two of my patients.

A look of genuine delight spreads across Sabina's face.

SCENE TEN

A conference room at the Park Hotel in Munich in November 1912. The meeting has just broken up, there are papers and half-empty carafes and glasses of water littering the green baize. Jung is on his feet, gathering his belongings together, while Freud is still in his position at the head of the table. Jung has clearly been lingering in the hope of speaking to Freud; but he's waiting for him to speak first: which he eventually does.

Freud Well, I think that was a very satisfactory session, don't you? I'd say we have every prospect of putting our enemies to rout.

Jung hesitates before answering.

Jung I was interested in what you said about monotheism: that historically it arose out of some kind of parricidal impulse.

Freud Well, yes: Akhnaton, who as far as we know was the first to put forward the bizarre notion that there was only one God, also had his father's name erased and chiselled out of all public monuments.

Jung Well, that's fascinating, if not strictly true.

Freud pauses in the act of tidying his papers. He looks up at Jung, a ferocious glint in his eye.

Freud Not true?

Jung No.

Freud You mean in the sense that it's most probably a myth?

Jung No, I mean there were two perfectly straightforward reasons for Akhnaton, or Amenhopis IV, as I prefer to call him, to excise his father's, or, more accurately, part of his father's name from the cartouches. First, this was something traditionally done by all new kings, who didn't wish their fathers' names to continue to be public currency.

Freud You mean in much the same say as your article in the *Yearbook* fails to mention my name?

The atmosphere is electric now. Jung hesitates before answering, trying to control his mounting indignation.

Jung No, it's not at all the same thing. If I failed to mention your name, it could only be because it's so well known, it hardly seems necessary.

Freud I see. Do go on.

Jung Secondly, Amenhopis only struck out the first half of his father, Amenhotep's, name, because, like the first half of his own name, it was shared by one of the gods, Amon, he was determined to eliminate.

Freud As simple as that?

Jung The explanation doesn't seem to me unduly simple.

Freud And you think your man, whatever you call him, felt no hostility whatsoever towards his father?

Jung I've no means of proof, of course. For all I know, Amenhopis may have thought his father's name was quite well known enough and that now it might be time to make a name for himself.

At which point, Freud, who during these last exchanges has looked increasingly pale and strained, faints again; this time sliding forward, ricocheting off the table and ending in a heap on the floor. Jung bounds forward, straightens him out and then lifts him in his arms, carries him across the room and lowers him gently onto a sofa. As he's lowering him, Freud comes to: he looks up at Jung, fear and vulnerability openly expressed on his face. Once he's settled him comfortably, Jung fetches a glass of water.

Jung Are you all right?

Freud How sweet it must be to die.

He takes the water and sips at it; then hands the glass back to Jung. His expression has hardened.

Thank you. Will you leave me now?

Jung I think perhaps I should stay until . . .

Freud Go.

Jung straightens up: without a word he turns and moves away, setting the glass down on the table. He's almost at the door, when Freud speaks again.

Take your freedom.

81

Jung stops; he doesn't turn round.

Jung What did you say?

Freud Spare me your pretence of friendship.

Jung turns to look at him.

For a long time now, our relationship has been hanging by a thread; and a thread, moreover, mostly consisting of past disappointments. We have nothing to lose by cutting it. I'm sure you agree.

Jung is struggling desperately to maintain his equanimity; but when he speaks, his voice is trembling.

Jung Very well: the rest is silence.

He turns and leaves the room: alone, Freud pauses, a hand over his face.

SCENE ELEVEN

The stage opens up, as much as possible, to reveal an idyllic scene: the beautiful garden at Künsnacht, sloping down to the dazzling blue of Lake Zürich on a perfect summer afternoon in 1913. The wine-red sails of Jung's boat are visible. Jung himself sits in a wicker chair angled to look out across the lake. Closer to us are Emma Jung and Agathe, who stand talking to Sabina, who now wears a wedding ring and is unmistakably pregnant.

Emma So good to have met you after all this time, Dr Spielrein.

Sabina We did meet once before. When I was your husband's patient.

Emma I think you're right.

Sabina Your children are glorious. (*She ruffles Agathe's golden hair.*)

Emma Thank you. You must let us know when yours arrives. I expect you want a boy.

Sabina No, no: my husband and I both think we would prefer a girl.

Emma Really. (*She turns to Agathe.*) Run along with the others now, darling.

Agathe Can't I stay?

Emma Now, do as you're told, or Dr Spielrein will stop wanting to have a little girl.

Agathe Oh, look, a butterfly.

She runs off after the butterfly; and Emma turns to Sabina.

Emma I wish you could help him.

Sabina Why, what's the matter?

Emma He's not himself. He's very confused and bogged down with his book. He's not sleeping. He's not taking on any new patients. I've been around this kind of thing enough to feel pretty confident that he's heading for a nervous breakdown.

Sabina I had no idea. What you're describing is so unlike my memory of him.

Emma If you were staying and not just passing through, I think I'd try to persuade him to let you analyse him. I know he . . . always set great store by your opinion.

Sabina turns to look across at him, concerned. Then she turns back to Emma.

Sabina This must be a great strain on you.

Emma Oh, well, it's not so very different . . . since he's started to withdraw, what's been happening has just confirmed what I've always assumed.

Sabina What's that?

Emma Oh, I've always known I don't have any real friends: just the people who are interested in him.

Sabina I'm sure that's not true.

Emma I don't mind. When they did come around, I always had to be careful not to say anything too intelligent, in case it took the attention away from him.

Sabina's at a loss to know what to say to this.

It doesn't matter. I always knew what I was getting into.

Jung raises his head and looks across at them.

You'd better go and talk to him. I know you'll be discreet.

Sabina Of course.

Emma Agathe!

She's about to move off, when Sabina stops her.

Sabina No one can help him more than you.

Emma I hope you're right.

Sabina leans forward and kisses her on both cheeks. Then, as Emma collects Agathe and sets off back into the house, Sabina moves over to join Jung. She tries not to react to his almost hostile expression. He looks gaunt and strained.

Sabina You have beautiful children.

Jung doesn't appear to have registered this remark. Instead, he surges abruptly to his feet.

84

Jung So, you're married.

Sabina Yes.

Jung And he's a doctor?

Sabina Yes. His name is Pavel Scheftel.

Jung Russian?

Sabina Yes, a Russian Jew.

Jung What's he like?

Sabina He's a kind man.

Jung Good, good. (*But he looks away, a spasm of pain crossing his face.*)

Sabina Are you all right?

Jung Oh, yes. I haven't been sleeping very well.

Sabina Oh?

Jung I keep having this recurring apocalyptic dream.

Sabina Can you describe it?

Jung A terrible flood covering the whole of northern Europe, from the North Sea to the Alps: houses washed away, thousands of floating corpses. Eventually, it arrives here, crashing down into the lake in a great tidal wave; and by this time the water, roaring down like some vast avalanche, has turned into blood. The blood of Europe.

Sabina What do you think it means?

Jung I've no idea: unless it's about to happen. Afterwards I feel sick; and ashamed. (*He turns away to look out across the lake; then back to Sabina.*) What are your plans?

Sabina We're thinking of going back to Russia: there's an enormous amount of work to do there.

Jung As long as you leave Vienna.

Sabina I spoke to him last week. I still can't accept there's nothing to be done to . . .

Jung There's nothing to be done. Looking back on it, I should have known, that day he refused to discuss a dream with me on the grounds that it might risk his authority. After that, for me, he had no authority. I don't mind telling you, it was a blow when I discovered you'd chosen his side.

Sabina It's not a question of sides. I have to work in the direction my instinct tells my intellect is the right one. Don't forget, I was cured by his method. And your differences are not as great as you both think. If you could find a way to advance together, it would be the most immense benefit to all of us.

Jung Is that what you came here to say?

Sabina No. I was passing through from Geneva. Naturally, I thought I would stop and visit. I have to go for my train very soon.

Jung Yes, of course, I'm sorry, I'm not . . . (*He breaks off, looks out across the lake again.*) It can't be done. What he'll never accept is that what we *understand* has got us nowhere. We have to go further, into uncharted territory. We have to go back, to the sources of everything we believe, before we can go forward. I don't just want to open a door and show the patient his illness, squatting there, like a toad. I want to find a way to help the patient reinvent himself, to send him off on a journey, at the end of which is waiting the person he was always intended to be.

Sabina But you mustn't make yourself ill in the process.

Jung Only the wounded physician can hope to heal.

Silence. Sabina breaks it, her tone calm.

Sabina I'm told you have a new mistress.

Jung Is that right?

Sabina Is she like me?

Jung No.

Sabina She's Jewish.

Jung Yes.

Sabina And she's an ex-patient.

Jung Yes.

Sabina Training to be an analyst.

Jung Yes.

Sabina But she's not like me?

Jung Naturally, she makes me think of you.

Sabina How does it work? How do you make it work?

Jung I don't know. Emma, as you've seen, is the foundation of my house; Toni is the perfume in the air. (*He turns to her.*) My love for you was the most important thing in my life. It made me understand who I am, for better or worse.

Sabina's expression, formerly sceptical, has softened; and her eyes fill with tears. Jung reaches out and rests a hand on her stomach for a second.

This should be mine.

Sabina Yes.

Jung But sometimes you have to do something unforgivable, just to be able to go on living.

And with that, he leans forward and kisses her gently on the forehead. Then he turns away and sets off, back towards his chair. Sabina hesitates a moment; then she turns and leaves the garden, touched by what he's said, though calm and not, for the moment, unhappy.

From his chair, Jung watches her leave. Then he turns back to the ethereally tranquil lake, turning golden in the setting sun. And as he sits, looking out across the water, and the lights slowly begin to fade, there's the sound, growing loud and louder, of some vast avalanche, crashing down the mountain into the unmoved depths.